More Poetry for Holidays

Selected by Nancy Larrick

Drawings by Harold Berson

GARRARD PUBLISHING COMPANY
CHAMPAIGN, ILLINOIS

SPECIAL DAYS AND HOLIDAYS

Every day is a special day for someone. Perhaps it is a birthday or the start of vacation. It may be a day that has become special through years of celebration like Halloween or Valentine's Day. Some of these special days have become legal holidays, when banks and stores are closed. These are red-letter days on the calendar.

Some days are also set aside for religious celebrations like Hanukkah or Christmas.

More Poetry for Holidays is a collection of poems about these special days and holidays. The poems are arranged in calendar order, beginning with New Year's Day. In the back of the book, there are notes about these special days, arranged alphabetically beginning with April Fools' Day.

Happy days!

Nancy Larrick

Library of Congress Cataloging in Publication Data
Larrick, Nancy, comp.
  More poetry for holidays.
  (Reading shelf series, poetry)
  SUMMARY: A collection of poems and rhymes for various holidays throughout the year. Includes a brief explanation of each holiday.
  1. Holidays — Juvenile poetry. [1. Holidays — Poetry] I. Berson, Harold, illus. II. Title.
PZ8.3.L328Mo   811'.008'033   73–6806
ISBN 0–8116–4116–3

The editors and publisher acknowledge with thanks permission received to reprint the poems in this collection.

Acknowledgments and formal notices of copyright for all material under copyright appear on pages 61 and 62, which are hereby made an extension of the copyright page.

Copyright © 1973 by Nancy Larrick Crosby
All rights reserved. Manufactured in the U.S.A.
International Standard Book Number: 0–8116–4116–3
Library of Congress Catalog Card Number: 73–6806

Contents

New Year's Day 5
Ground Hog Day 6
Pancake Day 7
Lincoln's Birthday 8
Valentine's Day 10
Washington's Birthday 14
St. Patrick's Day 16
Purim 18
Passover 19
April Fools' Day 20
Good Friday 21
Easter 22
Arbor Day 24
Bird Day 27
May Day 29
Summer Reading 31
Fourth of July 32
End of Vacation 33
Rosh Hashanah 34
Halloween 36
Children's Book Week 40
Sukkot 41
Thanksgiving 43
Hanukkah 45
Christmas 48
End of the Year 53
Special Days Have Special Meaning . . . 54
Index of Authors and Titles 63

New Year's Day

The Snowman's Resolution

The snowman's hat was crooked
and his nose was out of place
and several of his whiskers
had fallen from his face,

But the snowman didn't notice
for he was trying to think
of a New Year's resolution
that wouldn't melt or shrink.

He thought and planned and pondered
with his little snowball head
till his eyes began to glisten
and his toes began to spread;

At last he said, "I've got it!
I'll make a firm resolve
that no matter WHAT the weather
my smile will not dissolve."

Now the snowman acted wisely
and his resolution won,
for his splinter smile was WOODEN
and it didn't mind the sun.

Aileen Fisher

Ground Hog Day

To the Ground Hog

Will you
    Won't you
See your shadow?

Will it
    Won't it
Really matter?

Do you
    Don't you
Grin to see

People
    Take you
Seriously?

Kay Winters

Pancake Day

Mix a Pancake

Mix a pancake,
Stir a pancake,
　　Pop it in the pan;
Fry the pancake,
Toss the pancake,—
　　Catch it if you can.

Christina Rossetti

Lincoln's Birthday

To Meet Mr. Lincoln

If I lived at the time
That Mr. Lincoln did,
And I met Mr. Lincoln
With his stovepipe lid

And his coalblack cape
And his thundercloud beard,
And worn and sad-eyed
He appeared:

"Don't worry, Mr. Lincoln,"
I'd reach up and pat his hand,
"We've got a fine president
For this land;

And the Union will be saved,
And the slaves will go free;
And you will live forever
In our nation's memory."

Eve Merriam

Lincoln Monument: Washington

Let's go see old Abe
Sitting in the marble and the moonlight,
Sitting lonely in the marble and the moonlight,
Quiet for ten thousand centuries, old Abe.
Quiet for a million, million years.

Quiet—

And yet a voice forever
Against the
Timeless walls
Of time—
Old Abe.

Valentine's Day

Good Morning

Good morning to you, Valentine;
Curl your locks as I do mine,
One before and two behind,
Good morning to you, Valentine.

Traditional English Rhyme

Valentine

I got a valentine from Timmy
                             Jimmy
                             Tillie
                             Billie
                             Nicky
                             Micky
                             Ricky
                             Dicky
                             Laura
                             Nora
                             Cora
                             Flora
                             Donnie
                             Ronnie
                             Lonnie
                             Connie
                             Eva even sent me two
                             But I didn't get *none* from you!

                                         Shel Silverstein

My Valentine

I will give my love an apple
    without any core,
I will give my love a house
    without any door,
I will give my love a palace
    wherein she may be
And she may unlock it
    without any key.

How can there be an apple
    without any core?
How can there be a house
    without any door?
How can there be a palace
    wherein she may be
And she may unlock it
    without any key?

My head is an apple
    without any core,
My mind is a house
    without any door,
My heart is a palace
    wherein she may be
And she may unlock it
    without any key.

Old English Folk Song

Washington's Birthday

George Washington

George Washington is tops with me,
For he cut down the cherry tree,
And freed us from the British rule;
And helped us all stay home from school.

Shel Silverstein

Which Washington?

There are many Washingtons:
Which one do you like best?
The rich man with his powdered wig
And silk brocaded vest?

The sportsman from Virginia
Riding with his hounds,
Sounding a silver trumpet
On the green resplendent grounds?

The President with his tricorn hat
And polished leather boots,
With scarlet cape and ruffled shirts
And fine brass-buttoned suits?

Or the patchwork man with ragged feet,
Freezing at Valley Forge,
Richer in courage than all of them—
Though all of them were George.

Eve Merriam

St. Patrick's Day

When Irish hearts are happy,
Sure the world is bright and gay,
And when Irish eyes are shining
Sure they'll steal the heart away.

Irish Folk Song

Riggedy, higgedy, wiggedy, rig,
Paddy dances an Irish jig,
While feeding potatoes to his pig,
Riggedy, higgedy, wiggedy, rig.
Out goes Y-O-U.

Irish Counting-Out Game

I'll Wear a Shamrock

St. Patrick's day is with us,
The day when all that's seen
To right and left and everywhere
Is green, green, green!

And Irish tunes they whistle
And Irish songs they sing,
Today each Irish lad walks out
As proud as any king.

I'll wear an Irish shamrock
In my coat, the glad day through,
For my father and mother are Irish
And I am Irish, too!

Mary Carolyn Davies

Purim

Baking a Hamantash

Pat-a-cake, pat-a-cake,
Baker's man,
Bake me a *Hamantash*
Fast as you can!
Roll it, and fold it,
And make corners three;
Make one for mommy, for daddy and me!
Pat-a-cake, pat-a-cake,
Nice baker's man,
Bake me a *Hamantash*
Fast as you can!

Sara G. Levy

Passover

Passover Night

A moon, brimful of light,
Hangs in the cool sky,
And the new, polished stars
Glitter near it.
Over the wide fields
Blows the quiet wind,
Fragrant with new grass,
Snowdrops, crocuses.
Spring has come,
And with it
The glad night of honey and wine
And unleavened bread.

Edna Bockstein

April Fools' Day

Oh Did You Hear?

Oh did you hear?
The President has measles,
The Principal has just burned down the school,
Your hair is filled with jam and purple weasels

April Fool!

Shel Silverstein

Good Friday

Hot cross buns!
Hot cross buns!
One a penny, two a penny,
Hot cross buns!
If your daughters do not like them
Give them to your sons;
But if you haven't any of these pretty little elves
You cannot do better than eat them yourselves.

Old London Street Cry

Easter

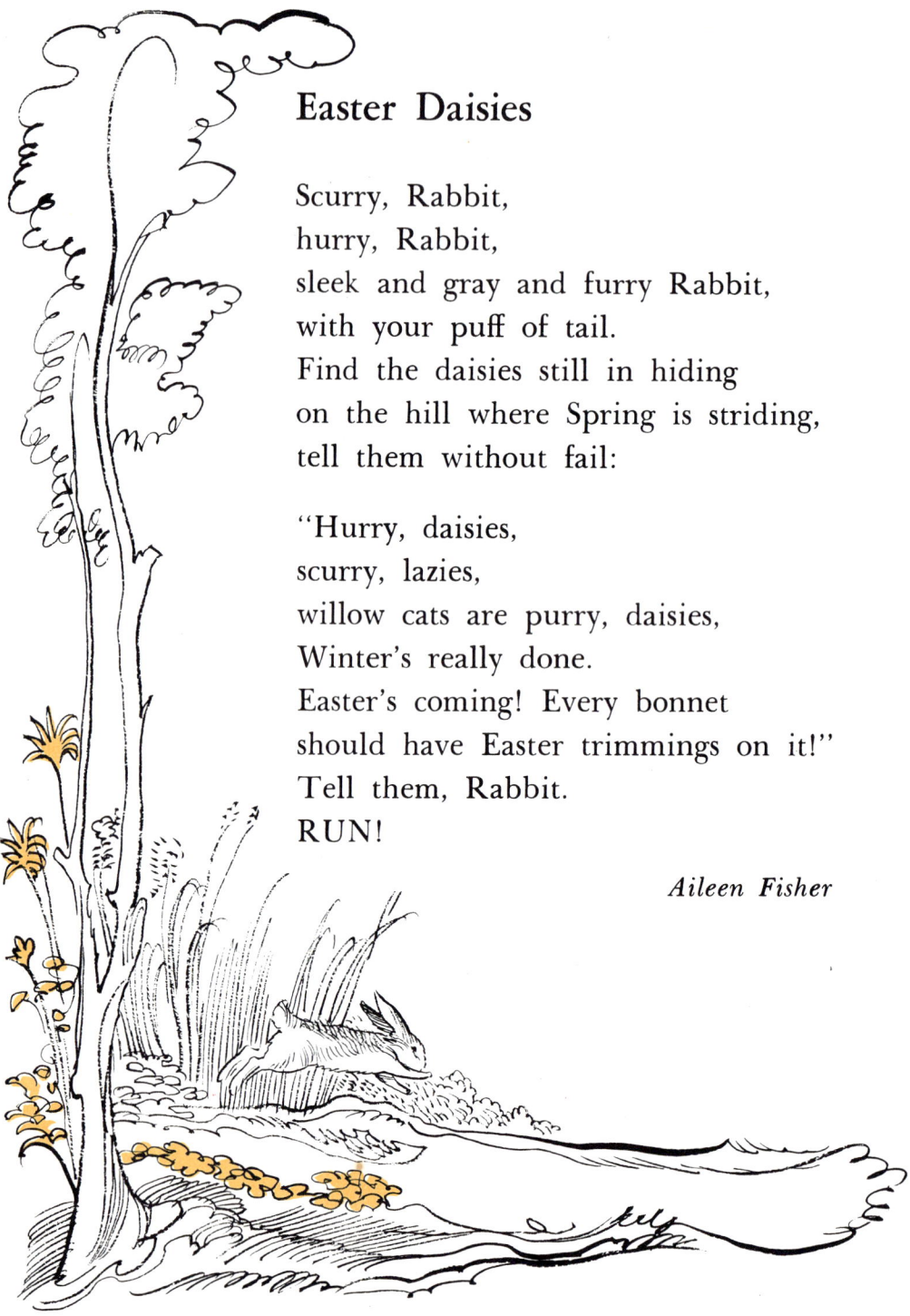

Easter Daisies

Scurry, Rabbit,
hurry, Rabbit,
sleek and gray and furry Rabbit,
with your puff of tail.
Find the daisies still in hiding
on the hill where Spring is striding,
tell them without fail:

"Hurry, daisies,
scurry, lazies,
willow cats are purry, daisies,
Winter's really done.
Easter's coming! Every bonnet
should have Easter trimmings on it!"
Tell them, Rabbit.
RUN!

Aileen Fisher

From ...

Listen, Rabbit

"Listen, rabbit,
with such tall ears
you hear more
than *anyone* hears.

"With two antennae
sticking up high
bringing you news
of earth and sky,
maybe you even
hear harebells ringing,
dogwood barking,
and larkspur singing."

Aileen Fisher

Arbor Day

Trees

Trees are the kindest things I know,
They do no harm, they simply grow

And spread a shade for sleepy cows,
And gather birds among their boughs.

They give us fruit in leaves above,
And wood to make our houses of,

And leaves to burn on Hallowe'en,
And in the Spring new buds of green.

They are the first when day's begun
To touch the beams of morning sun,

They are the last to hold the light
When evening changes into night,

And when a moon floats on the sky
They hum a drowsy lullaby

Of sleepy children long ago . . .
Trees are the kindest things I know.

Harry Behn

When I see the pine trees,
Standing along the road in a row,
It is like those,
Whom I left at home,
Seeing me off!

*Unknown Japanese poet
of the 7th or 8th century*

The Maple

In our big maple tree
There's a platform Father made,
And little seats high in the boughs
Where, in the deepest shade,
Inside the great, green thimble
My friends can climb with
        me
To sit a while and whisper
Within the whispering tree.

Elizabeth Coatsworth

Bird Day

Winter Birds

I can't go visit a snowbird—
I don't know where he stays.

I can't go visit a chickadee—
he has such flitty ways.

I can't go visit a bluejay
atop a snowy tree,

And so I scatter seeds around
and have them visit *me*.

Aileen Fisher

The owl hooted
Telling of the morning star.
He hooted again,
Announcing the dawn.

Yuma Indian Chant

A Robin

I wonder how
a robin hears?

I never yet
have seen his ears.

But I have seen him
cock his head,

And pull a worm
right out of bed.

Aileen Fisher

May Day

May Song

Spring is coming, spring is coming,
    Birdies, build your nest;
Weave together straw and feather,
    Doing each your best.

Spring is coming, spring is coming,
    Flowers are coming too;
Pansies, lilies, daffodillies,
    Now are coming through.

Spring is coming, spring is coming,
    All around is fair;
Shimmer and quiver on the river,
    Joy is everywhere.

Old English Country Rhyme

From...

The May Queen

"But I must gather knots of flowers
    and buds and garlands gay,
For I'm to be Queen o' the May, mother,
    I'm to be Queen o' the May."

Alfred Tennyson

Summer Reading

Summer Doings

Some at beaches
 Are sand-castling;
Some are silly—
Fighting, rasseling!

Some are swimming,
 Camping, hiking;
Some say stick-ball
 Is their liking.

Some on bikes are
 Gaily speeding;
Some are smarter—
 SUMMER READING!

William Cole

Fourth of July

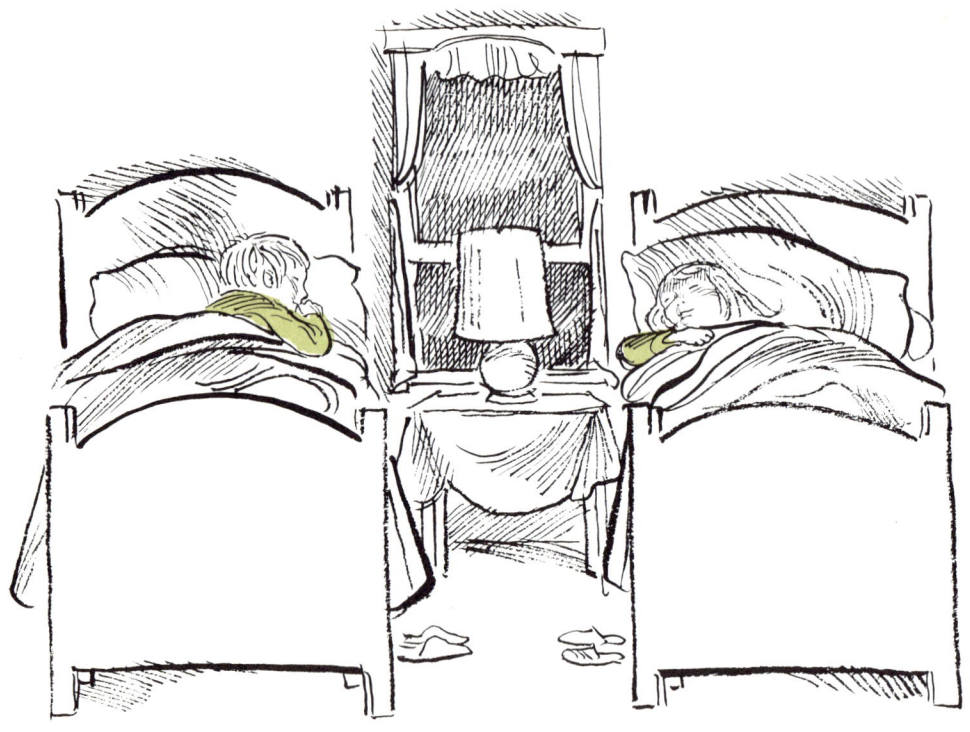

Fourth of July

Fat torpedoes in bursting jackets,
Firecrackers in scarlet packets.
We'll be up at crack o'day.
Fourth of July—Hurrah! Hooray!

Rachel Field

End of Vacation

Leavetaking

Vacation is over;
It's time to depart.
I must leave behind
(although it breaks my heart)

Tadpoles in the pond,
A can of eels,
A leaky rowboat,
Abandoned car wheels;

For I'm packing only
Necessities:
A month of sunsets
And two apple trees.

Eve Merriam

Rosh Hashanah

Rosh Hashanah

There was a sound so sweet and clear
It said to me, "The New Year's here."

It said, "Remember to be brave."
It said, "Remember to be good."

And when I heard the *shofar's* call
I stood up straight and said I would.

Ben Aronin

For a Good and Sweet New Year

Bees, bees,
Give us your honey!
Give us your honey, please.
We have special round bread,
Apples, too, round and red,
That came from the orchard trees.
We'll eat them with honey,
All golden and sunny,
When Rosh Hashanah is here;
Honey, apples, and bread
When the blessing is said
For a good and sweet New Year.

Sadie Rose Weilerstein

Halloween

A Prayer for Halloween

From Ghoulies and Ghosties,
Long-leggety Beasties,
And THINGS
That go BUMP in the night,
Good Lord, deliver us!

Unknown

A-Ha!

Whatever is inside that sheet
Just gave a dreadful shout!

A-ha, but what about those feet
That I see sticking out?

They help me guess who's hiding there,
Whose eyes are peeking through:

And how could anyone be scared
Of You!

Dorothy Aldis

From...
Knitted Things

There was a witch who knitted things:
Elephants and playground swings.
She knitted rain,
She knitted night,
But nothing really came out right.
The elephants had just one tusk
And night looked more
Like dawn or dusk.

Karla Kuskin

From . . .

The Witch of Willowby Wood

There once was a witch of Willowby Wood,
and a weird wild witch was she,
with her hair that was snarled
and hands that were gnarled,
and a kickety, rickety knee.
She could jump, they say
to the moon and back,
but this I never did see.

Rowena Bennett

Witches

      A star-white sky
Trees rustling as the wind lulls them to sleep
Shadowy creatures slinking through the grass
Clouds sailing,
Tattered and torn
Ragged and ripped.
Suddenly
In the sky
Soaring
    Zooming
        Diving about
           Flittering
Swooping into the air
Come witches
Cloaks ragged and torn
Streaming behind.
Cackling, laughing
Fading into darkness.

Linden, Age 10
New Zealand

Children's Book Week

Books make me feel like
>Flowers blooming in the summer air
>A beautiful dream
>Sunny rabbits
>A sound of music
>The world floating in my eyes
>Ten million dollars
>Adventure to an unknown land
>Having fun over a nice summer day
>Jumping in the leaves
>I'm swaying in the sky
>Birds flying in the sky
>Turning pages in my dreams.

>>*Fourth graders*
>>*Shirley Khabbaz, teacher*
>>*Springfield Elementary School*
>>*Pleasant Valley, Pa.*

Sukkot

From . . .
My Succah

I build again,
Of fragrant wood,
The hut that in
The desert stood.

Green boughs roof me
From the sky,
Light and shadow
Dance and fly.

The oranges hang
Overhead
Little suns of
Golden red.

The yellow pears and
Grapes of jet
Shimmer from
Their leafy net.

I keep my house
For seven days;
For seven nights
I offer praise

To Him who gave
His homeless brood
Huts for shelter,
Manna-food.

Edna Bockstein

Succah

There is the Succah, not yet covered,
All bare,
Standing alone in the field over there.
Soon it will be covered with greens
And some birds
With branches and fruits and berries
And ferns.
Now it is a Succah and the sun is
Shining through
The branches and berries, fruits
And ferns too.
Soon it will be over and the
Succah will be bare
Standing in the field alone,
Over there.

Elizabeth Wexler

Thanksgiving

We Thank Thee

For flowers that bloom about our feet;
For tender grass, so fresh, so sweet;
For song of bird, and hum of bee;
For all things fair we hear or see,
    Father in heaven, we thank Thee.

For blue of stream and blue of sky;
For pleasant shade of branches high;
For fragrant air and cooling breeze;
For beauty of the blooming trees,
    Father in heaven, we thank Thee.

Ralph Waldo Emerson

The lands around my dwelling
Are more beautiful
From the day
When it is given to me to see
Faces I have not seen before.
All is more beautiful,
All is more beautiful,
And life is Thankfulness.
These guests of mine
Make my house grand.

Eskimo Tribal Chant

Hanukkah

From . . .

Eight Are the Lights

Eight are the lights
    Of Chanuko
We light for a week
    And a day.
We kindle the lights,
    And bless the Lord,
And sing a song,
    And pray.

Eight are the lights
    Of Chanuko
For *justice* and *mercy*
    And *love*,
For *charity, courage*
    And *honor* and *peace*,
And *faith* in Heaven
    Above.

Ilo Orleans

Dreidel Song

Twirl about, dance about,
    Spin, spin, spin!
Turn, Dreidel, turn—
    Time to begin!

Soon it is Hanukkah—
    Fast, Dreidel, fast!
For you will lie still
    When Hanukkah's past.

Efraim Rosenzweig

Chanukah Poem

The smell of burned-out candles—
The sight of wrapped-up presents—
The feel of surprise—
The sound of dreidels spinning—
The taste of sizzling lotkas.
Chanukah is full of fun!

E-1 Class
Jewish Children's School
of Philadelphia

Christmas

Christmas Shoppers

Oh, the wind is brisk and biting
and the cold is not inviting,
but there's music, merry music everywhere.
The streets are full of bustle
and our feet are full of hustle,
for there's Christmas, merry Christmas in the air.

Oh, the wind is cold and chilly
and it whistles at us shrilly,
but there's music, merry music everywhere.
The bells are full of ringing
and our hearts are full of singing,
and there's Christmas, merry Christmas in the air.

Aileen Fisher

Day Before Christmas

We have been helping with the cake
    And licking out the pan,
And wrapping up our packages
    As neatly as we can.
And we have hung our stockings up
    Beside the open grate.
And now there's nothing more to do
    Except
        to
            wait!

Marchette Chute

Fir Tree Tall

Fir
tree tall
Lights glittering
Bright tinsel hung
Shimmering, glimmering
Laughter shining in the eyes
of boys
and girls
Lovely lovely
Christmas tree.

Joan Hanson

Merry Christmas

I saw on the snow
when I tried my skis
the track of a mouse
beside some trees.

Before he tunneled
to reach his house
he wrote "Merry Christmas"
in white, in mouse.

Aileen Fisher

When Christmas Comes

Take up the nets from lake and sea!
When Christmas comes let fish swim free.
Take up the traps and wily snares!
Let them have peace, the hunted hares.

Let all the creatures sport and play
in peace and trust on Christmas Day,
In honor of the humble child
who loved them all, the tame and wild.

Aileen Fisher

End of the Year

End of a Year

spring to summer,
summer to fall,
goodbye, oh year,
goodbye;
fall to winter,
winter to spring,
(one more time for the birds to sing,
one more day for the earth to bloom,
one time yet for the burning sun,
one more moment and then it's done,)
goodbye, oh year,
goodbye.

Patricia Hubbell

Special Days Have Special Meaning

APRIL FOOLS' DAY, April 1, is the day for practical jokes. The victim is called the April Fool. The custom is said to have originated in France and spread to England. In France the April Fool is called an April Fish.

ARBOR DAY is the official day for tree planting. It began in Nebraska, where April 22 is set aside as Arbor Day and is a legal holiday. On the first Arbor Day, in 1872, one million trees were planted in Nebraska. Now many states have an Arbor Day—the dates ranging from December to May.

BIRD DAY is a special day for learning about birds and how to protect them. The first Bird Day was celebrated in the schools of Oil City, Pennsylvania, in 1894. In some states Bird Day is April 26, the birthday of John James Audubon, the famous American naturalist and artist.

CHILDREN'S BOOK WEEK is set aside in November to create greater interest in books and reading. The first Children's Book Week was celebrated in 1919. Posters, streamers, and games for Book Week are distributed by the Children's Book Council, 175 Fifth Avenue, New York 10010.

CHRISTMAS DAY, December 25, is the Christian celebration of the birthday of Christ. It has grown into a season for elaborate decorations, gift giving, carol singing, and feasting.

EASTER is a Christian festival celebrating the resurrection of Christ. Its date varies each year but always falls between March 22 and April 25. It comes on the first Sunday after the first full moon following March 21.

THE FOURTH OF JULY is American Independence Day, the day on which the Declaration of Independence was adopted by the Continental Congress in 1776. In the past, the Fourth of July was celebrated by firing cannons, guns, rockets, and fireworks. Because there were many accidents, this practice is banned in most communities today.

GOOD FRIDAY is the Friday before Easter. It is the anniversary of the day on which Christ died on the cross. In honor of Good Friday, bakers make hot cross buns—each bun marked with a cross of white icing. Long ago English street vendors sold hot cross buns, using the familiar cry or chant, "Hot cross buns! Hot cross buns! One a penny, two a penny. Hot cross buns!"

GROUND HOG DAY, February 2, is the day when the ground hog or woodchuck is said to wake up from his long winter sleep to come out of his hole and look around. If the sun is shining and he sees his shadow, he is so frightened that he goes back in his hole. The legend is that there will then be six weeks of bad weather. If he does not see his shadow, he stays out and waits for the fair weather that is sure to come soon.

HALLOWEEN, meaning *hallowed evening,* is October 31, the night before All Saints' Day. Ancient legends suggest that on Halloween witches, ghosts, and spirits come out to scare people.

HANUKKAH (HAN-noo-kah) is the Jewish Feast of Lights or Dedication which begins on the twenty-fifth day of the Hebrew month of Kislev and lasts eight days. During Hanukkah, an eight-branch candlestick, or *menorah,* is lighted, one candle on the first evening, two on the second, and so on, until on the last evening all eight candles are lighted. The candles are lighted with a small torch called the *shamash.* Hanukkah, a time for gift giving, usually falls in the month of December. The *dreidel* is a top, the traditional toy given to children during Hanukkah. Hanukkah, meaning *dedication,* is sometimes called *Chanukah* or *Chanuko.*

LINCOLN'S BIRTHDAY, February 12, is a legal holiday in many states. Abraham Lincoln was born in 1809 in Hardin County, Kentucky. He served as President of the United States during the Civil War, from 1861 to 1865. The Lincoln Memorial in Washington is a beautiful white marble building showing a gigantic seated statue of Lincoln.

MAY DAY, the first day of May, is a time when the coming of spring is celebrated. Even the ancient Romans had May Day parades. In England it is the day to set up a Maypole, trimmed with flowers and ribbons, and have a May Day dance on the village green.

NEW YEAR'S DAY is the first day of the calendar year. According to our calendar—called the Gregorian calendar—New Year's Day is January 1. The Jewish New Year is celebrated in September or early October. (See Rosh Hashanah.) The Chinese New Year falls between January 21 and February 19.

PANCAKE DAY, or Shrove Tuesday, is the day before Ash Wednesday. Since it is the last day before the beginning of Lent, a period of fasting, Shrove Tuesday is a time for rich foods and sweets. Pancakes with sugar or syrup are traditional in England on Pancake Tuesday.

PASSOVER is the Jewish Festival of Freedom celebrating the Jews' escape from bondage in Egypt. It begins on the fifteenth day of the Hebrew month of Nisan and lasts eight days. This is in March or April in our calendar. At home Passover is celebrated with a feast called the *seder* (SAY-der). During the eight days of Passover, Jews eat *matzah,* an unleavened or "unraised" bread, to remind them of the kind of bread their ancestors took with them from Egypt.

PURIM (POO-rim) is a joyous Jewish festival which celebrates the delivery of the Jews of Persia (now Iran) from an evil plot to destroy them. It falls on the fourteenth day of the Hebrew month of Adar, generally in our month of March. A *hamantash* is a three-cornered Purim pastry filled with poppyseeds or jam.

ROSH HASHANAH (ROSH hah-SHAH-nah), the Jewish New Year, falls in September or early October. In many Jewish homes, the father repeats a blessing for a sweet year over an apple dipped in honey. Round, smooth loaves of bread represent the wish for a smooth year. The *shofar* is a trumpet, usually made of a curved ram's horn, used in the religious service of Rosh Hashanah.

ST. PATRICK'S DAY, March 17, is the day on which the patron saint of Ireland died in about 461. On that day Irish Americans wear a shamrock or something green, sing Irish songs, and in some cities stage elaborate parades to honor St. Patrick.

SUKKOT (sook-OHT), also called the Feast of Tabernacles, was celebrated by the ancient Hebrews as a festival of Thanksgiving at the end of the harvest season. It begins on the fifteenth day of the Hebrew month of Tishri and lasts nine days. During the festival, traditional Jews build a hut, called a *sukkah,* as a reminder of the huts or shelters their ancestors lived in while wandering through the wilderness. The sukkah is built with a slotted roof so that the stars can shine through. Then it is trimmed with green branches and fruits of the harvest. Another way of spelling the name of this festival is *Succot,* and the name of the hut, *succah*.

THANKSGIVING DAY is the fourth Thursday in November in the United States. Canada's Thanksgiving Day is the second Monday in October. On this day people give thanks with feasting and prayers. The first Thanksgiving in New England celebrated good crops and a bountiful harvest.

VALENTINE'S DAY, February 14, is not a legal holiday, but it is widely celebrated as a day to express affection and romance. Cards, gifts, and flowers are sent as valentines.

WASHINGTON'S BIRTHDAY, February 22, is a national holiday now celebrated on the third Monday of February. George Washington, the first president of the United States, was born in 1732 in Westmoreland County, Virginia.

Acknowledgments

Abelard-Schuman Limited: For "Easter Daisies" by Aileen Fisher. Copyright © 1933, 1938, 1946, 1958. Reprinted from *Runny Days, Sunny Days* by Aileen Fisher by permission of Abelard-Schuman Ltd., an Intext publisher.

Atheneum Publishers, Inc.: For "To Meet Mr. Lincoln" and "Which Washington?" by Eve Merriam from *There Is No Rhyme for Silver.* Copyright © 1962 by Eve Merriam. Used by permission of Atheneum Publishers. For "Leavetaking" by Eve Merriam, from *It Doesn't Always Have To Rhyme.* Copyright © 1964 by Eve Merriam. Used by permission of Atheneum Publishers. For "End of a Year" by Patricia Hubbell from *Catch Me a Wind.* Copyright © 1968 by Patricia Hubbell. Used by permission of Atheneum Publishers. For untitled Yuma Indian song, "The owl hooted," from *Songs of the Dream People: Chants and Images from the Indians and Eskimos of North America,* edited by James Houston. Copyright © 1972 by James Houston. Used by permission of Atheneum Publishers.

Behrman House, Inc.: For "Rosh Hashanah" reprinted from *Jolly Jingles for the Jewish Child,* Aronin, Ben. Behrman House, New York.

Bloch Publishing Co., Inc.: For "Baking a Hamantash" by Sara G. Levy. From *Mother Goose Rhymes for Jewish Children* by Sara G. Levy. Reprinted by permission of Bloch Publishing Co., New York.

Edna Bockstein: For "Passover Night" and "My Succah" by Edna Bockstein. Reprinted by permission of the author, who controls all rights.

Elizabeth Coatsworth: For "The Maple" by Elizabeth Coatsworth. Reprinted by permission of the author.

William Cole: For "Summer Doings" by William Cole. Copyright © 1971 by William Cole. Reprinted by permission of the author.

Thomas Y. Crowell Company: For "Merry Christmas," "Winter Birds," and "A Robin" by Aileen Fisher. From *Feathered Ones and Furry* by Aileen Fisher. Copyright © 1971 by Aileen Fisher. With permission of Thomas Y. Crowell Company, Inc., Publisher. For "Listen, Rabbit" from *Listen, Rabbit* by Aileen Fisher. Copyright © 1964 by Aileen Fisher. With permission of Thomas Y. Crowell Company, Inc., Publisher.

Doubleday & Company, Inc.: For "Fourth of July" by Rachel Field from *A Little Book of Days* by Rachel Field. Copyright © 1927 by Doubleday & Company, Inc. Reprinted by permission of Doubleday & Company, Inc.

E. P. Dutton & Co., Inc: For "Day Before Christmas" by Marchette Chute. Copyright © 1941 by Marchette Chute. Reprinted by permission of the author and E. P. Dutton & Co., Inc.

Aileen Fisher: For "Christmas Shoppers" and "When Christmas Comes" by Aileen Fisher. Reprinted by permission of the author, who controls all rights.

Grosset & Dunlap, Inc.: For "The Maple" by Elizabeth Coatsworth. Reprinted from *The Sparrow Bush, Rhymes* by Elizabeth Coatsworth. Text copyright © 1966 by Grosset & Dunlap, Inc. Illustrations Copyright © 1966 by Stefan Martin. Published by Grosset & Dunlap, Inc.

Joan Hanson: For "Fir Tree Tall" by Joan Hanson from *Concrete Is Not Always Hard,* edited by A. Barbara Pilon, Middletown, Conn.: Xerox Education Publications, 1972.

Harcourt Brace Jovanovich, Inc.: For "Trees" by Harry Behn. From *The Little Hill,* copyright © 1949, by Harry Behn. Reprinted by permission of Harcourt Brace Jovanovich, Inc.

Harper & Row Publishers, Inc.: For "Knitted Things" from *Alexander Soames: His Poems* by Karla Kuskin. Copyright © 1962 by Karla Kuskin. Reprinted by permission of Harper & Row.

Jewish Children's School of Philadelphia: For "Chanukah Poem" by E-1 Class, Jewish Children's School of Philadelphia, from *Jewish Children's Book of Philadelphia Yearbook 1972.* For "Succah" by Elizabeth Wexler, from *June 1972 Yearbook of the Jewish Children's School of Philadelphia,* copyright by Herman T. Wexler.

Alfred A. Knopf, Inc.: For "Lincoln Monument: Washington" by Langston Hughes. Copyright © 1932 by Alfred A. Knopf, Inc., and renewed 1960 by Langston Hughes. Reprinted from *The Dream Keeper and Other Poems*, by Langston Hughes, by permission of Alfred A. Knopf, Inc.

Longman Canada Limited: For untitled Yuma Indian song, "The owl hooted," from *Songs of the Dream People: Chants and Images from the Indians and Eskimos of North America*, edited by James Houston. Copyright © 1972 by James Houston. Published in the United States by Atheneum and published in Canada by Longman Canada Limited.

National Women's League of the United Synagogue of America: For "For a Good and Sweet New Year" from *The Singing Way: Poems for Jewish Children* by Sadie Rose Weilerstein. National Women's League of the United Synagogue of America, New York 1946.

Penguin Books, Ltd.: For "Witches" by Linden, age 10, New Zealand, from *Miracles: Poems by Children of the English Speaking World* collected by Richard Lewis. Copyright © Richard Lewis, 1966. Reprinted by permission of The Penguin Press, Allen Lane, Founder.

Plays, Inc., Publishers: For "The Witch of Willowby Wood" by Rowena Bennett. Reprinted from *Creative Plays and Programs for Holidays*, by Rowena Bennett. Plays, Inc., Publishers, Boston, Mass. 02116. Copyright © 1966 by Rowena Bennett. For "The Snowman's Resolution" by Aileen Fisher. Copyright © 1953 by Aileen Fisher. Reprinted from *Holiday Programs for Boys and Girls*, by Aileen Fisher. Plays, Inc., Publishers, Boston, Mass. 02116.

G. P. Putnam's Sons: For "A-Ha!" by Dorothy Aldis. Reprinted by permission of G. P. Putnam's Sons from *All Together* by Dorothy Aldis. Copyright © 1925, 1926, 1927, 1928, 1934, 1939, and 1952 by Dorothy Aldis.

Rand McNally & Company: For "I'll Wear a Shamrock" by Mary Carolyn Davies from *Child Life* Magazine, Copyright 1926, 1954 by Rand McNally & Company.

Shel Silverstein: For "Oh Did You Hear?," "George Washington," and "Valentine" by Shel Silverstein. Copyright © 1961 by Shel Silverstein. Reprinted by permission of Shel Silverstein.

Simon & Schuster, Inc.: "Witches" by Linden, from *Miracles: Poems by Children of the English Speaking World*, collected by Richard Lewis. Copyright © 1966 by Richard Lewis. Reprinted by permission of Simon and Schuster.

Springfield Elementary School, Fourth Graders: For "Books Make Me Feel Like" by Fourth Graders, Shirley Khabbaz, Teacher, Springfield Elementary School, Pleasant Valley, Pennsylvania. Reprinted by permission of the authors, who control all rights. Copyright © 1973.

Union of American Hebrew Congregations: For "Eight Are the Lights" by Ilo Orleans from *Within Thy Hand, My Poem Book of Prayers* by Ilo Orleans, and "Dreidel Song" by Efraim Rosenzweig from *Now We Begin* by Efraim Rosenzweig. Reprinted by permission of Union of American Hebrew Congregations.

Kay L. Winters: For "The Ground Hog," by Kay Winters. Reprinted by permission of the author, who controls all rights. Copyright © 1973.

The World Publishing Company: For "Eskimo Tribal Chant." Reprinted by permission of The World Publishing Company from *Beyond These High Hills: A Book of Eskimo Poems*, edited by Knud Rasmussen. Copyright © 1961 by The World Publishing Company.

Index of Authors and Titles

A-Ha! 36
Aldis, Dorothy
  A-Ha! 36
Aronin, Ben
  Rosh Hashanah 34

Baking a Hamantash 18
Behn, Harry
  Trees 24
Bennett, Rowena
  from *The Witch*
    of Willowby Wood 38
Bockstein, Edna
  from *My Succah* 41
  Passover Night 19
Books make me feel like 40

Chanukah Poem 47
Christmas Shoppers 48
Chute, Marchette
  Day Before Christmas 49
Coatsworth, Elizabeth
  The Maple 26
Cole, William
  Summer Doings 31

Davies, Mary Carolyn
  I'll Wear a Shamrock 17
Day Before Christmas 49
Dreidel Song 46

Easter Daisies 22
Eight Are the Lights, from 45
Emerson, Ralph Waldo
  We Thank Thee 43
End of a Year 53

Field, Rachel
  Fourth of July 32

Fir Tree Tall 50
Fisher, Aileen
  Christmas Shoppers 48
  Easter Daisies 22
  from *Listen, Rabbit* 23
  Merry Christmas 51
  A Robin 28
  The Snowman's Resolution 5
  When Christmas Comes 52
  Winter Birds 27
For a Good and Sweet New Year 35
Fourth of July 32

George Washington 14
Good Morning 10

Hanson, Joan
  Fir Tree Tall 50
Hot cross buns! 21
Hubbell, Patricia
  End of a Year 53
Hughes, Langston
  Lincoln Monument: Washington 9

I'll Wear a Shamrock 17

Jewish Children's School
of Philadelphia, E-1 Class
  Chanukah Poem 47

Knitted Things, from 37
Kuskin, Karla
  from *Knitted Things* 37

Leavetaking 33
Levy, Sara G.
  Baking a Hamantash 18
Lincoln Monument: Washington 9
Linden, Age 10, New Zealand
  Witches 39

Listen, Rabbit, from   23

Maple, The   26
May Queen, The   30
May Song   29
Merriam, Eve
   Leavetaking   33
   To Meet Mr. Lincoln   8
   Which Washington?   15
Merry Christmas   51
Mix a Pancake   7
My Succah, from   41
My Valentine   12

Oh Did You Hear?   20
Orleans, Ilo
   from *Eight Are the Lights*   45

Passover Night   19
Prayer for Halloween, A   36

Riggedy, higgedy, wiggedy, rig   16
Robin, A,   28
Rosenzweig, Efraim
   Dreidel Song   46
Rosh Hashanah   34
Rossetti, Christina
   Mix a Pancake   7

Silverstein, Shel
   George Washington   14
   Oh Did You Hear?   20
   Valentine   11
Snowman's Resolution, The   5
Springfield Elementary School,
Fourth Graders
   Books make me feel like   40
Succah   42
Summer Doings   31

Tennyson, Alfred
   from *The May Queen*   30
The lands around my dwelling   44
The owl hooted   28
To Meet Mr. Lincoln   8
To the Ground Hog   6
Trees   24
Unknown
   A Prayer for Halloween   36
   Good Morning   10
   Hot cross buns!   21
   May Song   29
   My Valentine   12
   Riggedy, higgedy, wiggedy, rig   16
   The lands around my dwelling   44
   The owl hooted   28
   When I see the pine trees   25
   When Irish hearts are happy   16

Valentine   11

We Thank Thee   43
Weilerstein, Sadie Rose
   For a Good and Sweet New Year
Wexler, Elizabeth
   Succah   42
When Christmas Comes   52
When I see the pine trees   25
When Irish hearts are happy   16
Which Washington?   15
Winter Birds   27
Winters, Kay
   To the Ground Hog   6
Witch of Willowby Wood, from *The*   38
Witches   39